D1249400

◂ UGANDA ▸

MAJOR WORLD NATIONS

UGANDA

Alexander Creed

CHELSEA HOUSE PUBLISHERS
Philadelphia

Chelsea House Publishers

Contributing Author: Tom Purdom

Copyright © 1999 by Chelsea House Publishers,
a division of Main Line Book Co.

First Printing

1 3 5 7 9 8 6 4 2

Library of Congress Cataloging-in-Publication Data

Creed, Alexander.
Uganda.
Includes index.

Summary: Surveys the history, topography, people,
and culture of Uganda, with an emphasis on its current
economy, industry, and place in the political world.

1. Uganda.   [1. Uganda]   I. Title.
DT433.222.C74   1987   967.6'1   87-11710

ISBN 0-7910-4770-9

◄ C O N T E N T S ►

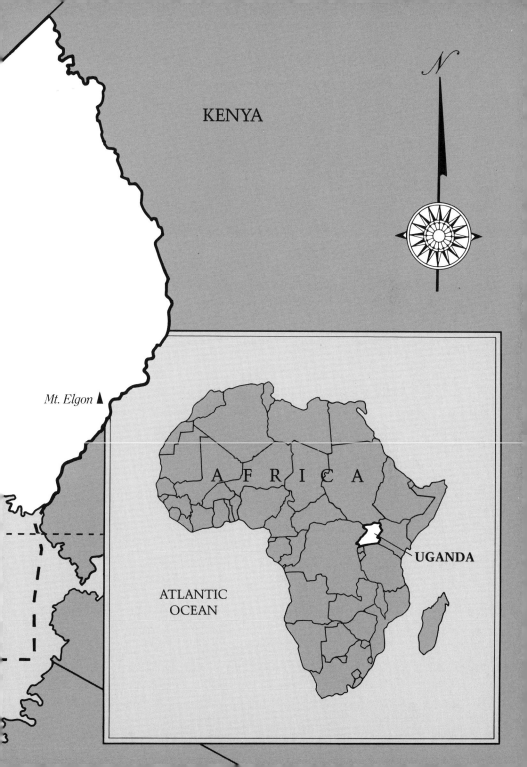

KENYA

N

Mt. Elgon ▲

A F R I C A

ATLANTIC
OCEAN

UGANDA

3

◄ FACTS AT A GLANCE ►

Land and People

Area	91,000 square miles (236,000 square kilometers)
Altitude	3,000 to 6,000 feet (900 to 1,800 meters)
Highest Point	Margherita Peak, 16,763 feet (5,110 m)
Major Lakes	Lake Victoria, Lake Albert, Lake Edward, Lake George
Population	20,100,000
Population Density	221 people per square mile (85 per sq km)
Capital	Kampala (population 773,000)
Other Major Cities	Jinja, Entebbe
Official Language	English
Other Languages	Luganda, Swahili, Bantu languages, Nilotic languages
Religions	Roman Catholic, 33 percent; Protestant, 33 percent; Islam, 16 percent; indigenous beliefs, 18 percent
Literacy Rate	62 percent
Average Life Expectancy	40 years
Infant Mortality Rate	99.4 deaths per 1,000 births

Economy

Resources	Copper, cobalt, limestone, salt
Employment	Agriculture, over 80 percent of population
Major Cash Crops	Coffee, tea, cotton, tobacco
Industries	Brewing, cotton textiles, cement
Currency	Ugandan shilling, divided into 100 cents
Per Capita Gross Domestic Product	Equal to U.S. $900

Government

Form of Government	Republic
Legislature	National Assembly with 276 members: 214 members are elected; 39 seats are reserved for indirectly elected women; 23 are set aside for indirectly elected representatives of other groups, including the army (10 members), the disabled (5), youth (5), and trade unions (3)
Head of State	President Yoweri Museveni
Eligibility to Vote	All citizens 18 years of age and older

◄HISTORY AT A GLANCE►

1400s   Tribal kingdoms based on agriculture arise.

1800s   The Buganda, Bagosa, Toro, and Ankole kingdoms are well-established.

1858   Englishman John Hanning Speke discovers Lake Victoria. Four years later, he discovers the source of the Nile River. During his travels, he meets Mutesa I, king of Buganda.

1893   The British East Africa Company claims Uganda.

1896   England takes control of the territory from the company and administers it as a protectorate. Alone among the tribes, the Buganda are allowed to keep their land.

1890s   England builds the East African railway connecting the Kenya coast to Uganda. The British introduce coffee and cotton cultivation. They also encourage Asians living in Uganda to develop industry and shopkeeping.

1897   Mwanza leads the first of four unsuccessful Buganda revolts against British rule.

1900   England grants the Buganda council of chiefs lawmaking and land ownership rights.

1939   Edward Frederick Mutesa II ascends to the Buganda throne.

1948   England establishes the East African High Commission to gain greater control of Uganda. Friction between tribal groups increases.

1950s	England supports efforts by some tribes to form a unified Ugandan nation. The Buganda oppose these efforts.
1953	Buganda leaders are deported to England.
1955	The Buganda king is allowed to return to Uganda. He pledges peace with the other tribes in exchange for Ugandan independence from England.
1962	Uganda declares independence. Apollo Milton Obote, an anti-Buganda, is elected prime minister.
1963	The Parliament elects Mutesa II president.
1966	Obote takes over the government and declares himself president. Mutesa II is exiled to London, England.
1967	Obote forms a new political party, the Uganda People's Congress. Mutesa II dies in London.
1969	Obote introduces Socialist programs.
1971	Idi Amin leads a military coup to overthrow Obote's government. His Suspension of Political Activities Decree takes away many civil rights from the people.
1972	Amin expels Israelis and Asians from Uganda.
1976	Israeli commandos capture a hijacked jet at Entebbe airport.
1978	Protesting violations of human rights, the United States ends trade with Uganda. Uganda raids neighboring Tanzania, but the Tanzanian army is victorious.
1979	Tanzanian forces advance on Kampala. The Ugandan people are highly discontented with their government. Idi Amin flees to Libya. The Ugandan National Liberation Front elects Yusufu Lule president, then deposes him. Godfrey Binaisa serves as president for several months.
1980	Obote returns from exile and takes control of the government. Uganda is plagued by tribal fighting,

severe economic depression, vandalism, and a famine that kills 30,000 people. Obote attacks Amin's home province. In the first general elections since 1962, Obote is elected president.

early 1980s   Obote's rule grows oppressive and militaristic. Antigovernment resistance movements form. Obote's soldiers massacre 500,000 villagers in the Luwero district.

1985   Army officer Tito Okello deposes Obote.

1986   Rebel leader Yoweri Museveni takes control of the government. National Resistance Council is formed. All activity by political parties is banned. Commissions investigate corruption and human rights violations. Eighty percent of the police force is dishonorably dismissed.

1987   National Resistance Council offers amnesty to rebels. Rebellion by the "Holy Spirit" movement is suppressed. Uganda negotiates economic policy framework with the International Monetary Fund and the World Bank and begins economic programs designed to increase incentives to the private sector and repair war damage.

1990   President Museveni is elected chairman of the Organization of African Unity (OAU), signaling Uganda's re-entry into the world community.

1995   A new constitution is adopted.

1996   First elections are held under new constitution. Museveni is elected president in May with 74 percent of vote. Legislative elections are held in June.

1997–1998   A guerrilla group called the Lord's Resistance Army stages raids in portions of northern Uganda.

In the heart of East Africa, Uganda is a land of forests, plains, mountains, and wildlife.

Uganda
and the World

Nestled in the heart of East Africa lies the Republic of Uganda—one of Africa's most beautiful and controversial lands. The small country boasts rich, fertile soil and a moderate climate favorable to a thriving agricultural economy. But decades of political turmoil and dictatorial regimes have prevented Uganda from achieving its full potential.

When European explorers and missionaries first came to East Africa in the late 1800s, a group of several tribal kingdoms occupied the region that is now known as Uganda. The largest tribal group was the Buganda kingdom. Friction among the tribes had long since created a climate of internal strife, and these tribal rivalries accelerated after Great Britain made part of Uganda a protectorate in 1894. The British allowed the Buganda kingdom to retain its traditional homeland, but they did not extend this right to other kingdoms. This increased the bad feeling among the tribes and kept them from uniting.

Political turmoil has continued to rock Uganda since it gained independence from Britain in 1962. The troubled country made world headlines in 1971, when Idi Amin overthrew the government of Prime Minister Milton Obote in a military coup.

Amin stunned the world with his domestic policies, reported to include severe human rights violations and even widespread mass murder.

A man kneels behind a voting booth in Kampala on May 9, 1996, the day Uganda held its first election under the new constitution.

Amin's actions strained relations with many nations, including the United States, Canada, and Great Britain.

In 1979, Tanzanian and exiled Ugandan troops overthrew Amin's regime. Milton Obote returned from exile and eventually set up another military dictatorship. Then, in 1986, a rebel leader named Yoweri Museveni overthrew Obote and established a stable government. In late 1995, almost a decade after Museveni took control, a new constitution went into effect. The next year, Uganda held its first democratic election since 1962, and Museveni received over 70 percent of the vote.

The Museveni government has stabilized the political situation in Uganda and given the country one of the highest economic growth rates in Africa. But the people of Uganda still face many challenges. Uganda remains a poor country, and the government continues to struggle with the problems created by guerrilla bands and by the spread of acquired immunodeficiency syndrome (AIDS). The nation is making progress, however, and Ugandans are beginning to feel they can achieve a brighter future.

*Savannas—broad plains of tall grass and scattered forest—cover much of the U*g
*countryside. Giraffes are among the dozens of animal species that roam the sav*a

The Cradle of the Nile

Uganda lies in East Africa on the equator, 500 miles (800 kilometers) west of the Indian Ocean. It is known as "The Cradle of the Nile" because the world's longest river originates at Lake Victoria, in Uganda's southeastern corner. The country's natural beauty has caused many world travelers, among them the young Winston Churchill, to call it the loveliest area in Africa and one of the most striking in the world.

Uganda is about the size of the state of Oregon, with a total area of 91,000 square miles (236,000 square kilometers). Water and swamps cover one-sixth of this land. The country is landlocked, so it ships exports through neighboring Kenya to the port of Mombasa, 500 miles (800 kilometers) east on the Indian Ocean. In addition to Kenya, Uganda shares borders with Sudan to the north, Congo (formerly Zaire) to the west, and Tanzania and Rwanda to the south.

Most of Uganda lies on the East African Plateau, ranging from 3,000 to 6,000 feet (900 to 1,830 meters) above sea level. Tall grass and scattered "islands" of low trees and shrubs cover large portions of the country. In the areas surrounding bodies of water, the land is often marshy and the grass is thicker and denser.

In parts of western Uganda, however, the terrain is desert-like. Here, rain rarely falls, and the only trees are acacias (which have yellow bark and flat tops), euphorbia trees (which look like cactus), and thornbushes. Visitors to these regions often remark that the landscape is similar to that of the American West. Except for an occasional giraffe or elephant, this arid land is deserted.

Mountains and Valleys

The mountain ranges on Uganda's eastern and western borders have some of the most spectacular peaks in the world. Uganda's most famous range is the Ruwenzori (also called the Mountains of the Moon), on the western border with Congo. One mountain peak in this range, Margherita Peak, atop Mount Stanley, is the tallest in the country, at 16,763 feet (5,110 meters).

The Ruwenzori Mountains were formed thousands of years ago when a severe earthquake left a huge crack on the surface of the earth, thrusting portions of land into great mountains and plateaus and causing other portions to sink into a deep valley. Today, this valley is called the Great Rift Valley. It stretches more than 4,000 miles (6,400 kilometers), starting in the Middle East, passing beneath the Red Sea, cutting diagonally across Ethiopia, and entering Kenya. At a point under Kenya's Lake Rudolf, the valley branches into two arms. The western branch forms Uganda's border with Congo.

Other mountains in Uganda are volcanic. On clear nights, flames from the Virunga range lick the pitch-black sky. In parts of Uganda, the land is scarred from the fiery debris of volcanic eruptions. The Mufumbiro Mountains, in the southwestern corner of Uganda, are a series of extinct volcanoes. At 13,550 feet (4,065 meters), Mount Mahavura is the highest peak in the Mufumbiro range. Today, the center of its gaping crater is a huge lake. During Uganda's rainy season, the lake overflows, trickling down the sides of the mountain and watering the land below. Mount Elgon, rising to 14,178 feet (4,253 m) on the eastern border with Kenya, is another extinct volcano. Mount Elgon measures nearly 50 miles (80 kilometers) across at the base, and its crater is 4 miles (6.4 km) across at the top.

Lakes and Rivers

Uganda has many lakes and rivers. Lake Victoria, at 26,828 square miles (69,485 square kilometers), is Africa's largest freshwater lake and the world's second largest. The lake covers Uganda's southeast corner and extends into Kenya and Tanzania.

Lake Victoria is a relatively shallow lake, dotted with dozens of tiny islands, particularly near the shoreline. For years, Ugandans have used Lake Victoria to transport products, such as cotton and coffee, from lakeside towns to the manufacturing centers of Kampala and Jinja. Tribespeople also travel on the lake from village to village. Lake Victoria provides a source of freshwater fish, such as lungfish and tilapatia. Because bacteria and disease-carrying parasites live in its waters, swimming is dangerous.

The great Nile River joins several of Uganda's major lakes. From its origin at Lake Victoria, the Nile begins its 4,000-mile (6,400-kilometer)

Boat races on one of the many rivers celebrate Uganda's independence in 1962.

course northward to the Mediterranean Sea. It first passes through Ripon Falls, where the Owen Falls Dam hydroelectric power plant harnesses the power of the water's force. After the falls, the river, known as the Victoria Nile at this point, flows into shallow and marshy Lake Kyoga. To the north of Kyoga, the river makes its way over the rapids of the Karuma Falls, then flows 40 miles (64 kilometers) west to Murchison Falls, where it cascades into a 20-foot- (6-meter-) wide cleft. The mist caused by the 140-foot (42-meter) drop looks almost like smoke. From Murchison Falls, the Victoria Nile enters Lake Albert, then flows into Sudan.

Lake Edward and Lake George are Uganda's two other major lakes. The two lakes are about 30 miles (50 kilometers) apart. Lake Edward forms part of the border with Congo. The Ugandan section of its shoreline is included in Uganda's most popular game preserve, Queen Elizabeth National Park. The park also protects the northern and western shores of Lake George.

Climate

Uganda has a tropical climate, with two rainy and two dry seasons each year. The first rainy season occurs from March through May, and the second one from August through November. The amount of rainfall varies by region. The northeastern region has a semi-arid climate and receives less than 20 inches (500 millimeters) of rain per year. The southwestern region gets more rain, as much as 50 inches (1,300 mm) or more a year. Thus, towns such as Entebbe, on Lake Victoria, have a lush, green countryside.

Uganda's elevation gives it a year-round temperate climate. Low temperatures average 60° Fahrenheit (16° Centigrade) and average highs seldom top 85° F (30° C).

Plant and Animal Life

Plant life in Uganda is abundant and varied. Vegetation benefits from the volcanic soil, which is nutrient-rich and favorable to growth. Banana trees grow throughout the country, along with tropical fruit such as passion fruit and mango. Ugandans use the banana tree and its fruit for food, beer, and even clothing. Other food-producing plants include cassava, sweet potatoes, peanuts, peas, and maize (corn).

Coffee plants thrive in Uganda's soil. Tea plants also grow well in the mountain highlands, and cotton, introduced at the turn of the century, now grows wild throughout the country. Beautiful flowers, including violets, scarlet lobelias, groundsels, and buttercups, abound on Uganda's mountain slopes. At lower elevations, orchids, hibiscus, jacaranda, and frangipani bloom throughout the year.

Many of the animals native to Africa live in Uganda. Among these are zebras and several varieties of antelope, including the dik-dik, which weighs only 8 to 10 pounds (3.6 to 4.5 kilograms). Lions, cheetahs, and leopards feed on these animals. Scavengers include jackals, hyenas, wild dogs, marabou storks, and vultures.

Giraffes roam the savannas, eating the leaves and branches of the acacia tree. Elephants feed mainly on grasslands and trees, and sometimes endanger their own survival by stripping entire areas bare. Park rangers periodically have to thin out the herds when the animals have nothing left to eat.

Hippopotamuses and rhinoceroses live along the banks of rivers and lakes. The white rhinoceros is native to the entire East African region, but the black rhinoceros, much rarer than its cousin, exists only in Uganda. Its broad mouth and square jaw make it look more like a hippopotamus. Confined mainly to the waters of the Albert Nile, it is considered an endangered species.

Monkeys and baboons thrive in the rural regions of Uganda. The gray velvet monkey has a black, heart-shaped face outlined in white. The rare colobus monkey has a coat of silky fur. For many years, villagers have used this fur for their elaborate tribal headdresses. Chimpanzees live in wooded areas throughout Uganda. Shy mountain gorillas live in the highlands of the southwestern region. So many of them have been used for medical research, however, that they are now on the endangered species list. Many have been taken to zoos throughout the world.

Uganda is home to many reptiles. Among the most notorious is the crocodile, which can grow up to 12 feet (3.6 meters) long. Deadly snakes, including pythons, puff adders, and cobras, are plentiful.

Bird life in Uganda is as varied as the wild game. The flightless ostrich is one of the largest birds in the world, and even though it cannot fly, it is a

A single herd of hungry elephants can strip an entire region of grass and leaves.

surprisingly fast runner. It can move at speeds of up to 45 miles (72 kilometers) an hour. Another unusual bird of the region is the secretary bird, which has white breast feathers, a black tail, and quills on either side of its head that make it look like a secretary with a pencil behind each ear.

The crane is the national bird and is pictured on the nation's flag. It has a black-and-white body, with a tufted crown of gold and red feathers. Other waterbirds are plentiful, too. Flamingos live in certain waters, partic-

Ten thousand termites may inhabit this sun-baked hill.

ularly those that are rich in salt. Marabou storks often prey on flamingo eggs and sometimes on baby flamingos. Smaller birds, such as the bishop bird, whose color resembles the scarlet of a bishop's robe, dart from bush to bush. Blue-and-copper-colored starlings inhabit all of Uganda's forests.

The honey guide bird is known for its ability to locate bees. Although it is unable to enter the beehive, it has helped tribespeople for hundreds of years and has spawned many legends. After the bird helps a tribe find honey, a tribesman is supposed to leave insect larvae or beeswax for it to eat. According to one legend, if the man fails to do this, the honey guide has the power to punish him by luring him into the forest and leading him to disaster and ruin.

Uganda has many national parks; among these are Murchison Falls (Kabalega) north of Jinga, Kidepo Valley on the Sudan border, and Queen Elizabeth (Ruwenzori) in the southwest. Animals and plants are protected in these areas, which are open to visitors.

Important Insects

Living in the brush and thickets of the forested areas, the dreaded tsetse fly looks like a large housefly with crossed wings. It lives on the blood of humans and domestic animals. Its bite can cause sleeping sickness and a similar disease called *nagana* in livestock. The tsetse fly is a major problem. It has hampered economic development in large regions of Africa. Several international organizations are helping local governments deal with it. The most important control methods are traps and the "sterile male" strategy—a technique that floods an area with male flies that have been sterilized with radiation. The female flies mate with the sterile males and die without reproducing.

Termite hills dot the land in the drier areas of Uganda. Composed of earth and partially digested wood, the hills are home to entire colonies of termites. Beneath the sun-baked surface of a termite hill may live as many as 10,000 insects. Termites fashion extremely sophisticated nests that include tunnels and galleries—and even little ducts that provide a natural cooling system. Inside, they grow fungus as a food source. It takes a termite colony only six months to construct a hill, which can be taller than a man. Unlike tsetse flies, termites are useful to Ugandans because they are a valuable food source. For the many people who live primarily on banana dishes, fried termites provide an important source of protein.

The British explorer John Hanning Speke discovered Lake Victoria.

A Troubled History

Uganda was not always a single nation. It began as a group of many tribal kingdoms, all sharing the same land. Age-old rivalries between neighboring tribes continue today, and this internal fighting has contributed to Uganda's political troubles in recent years.

Unlike the people of other African areas, the early tribes of Uganda were not forced to wander to find water and food. The fertile soil and ready water supply allowed many edible plants to grow. As a result, the tribes were able to settle in one place, where they developed advanced cultures. Most of the early tribal kingdoms developed sometime during the 1400s. By the 1800s, kingdoms such as Basoga, Buganda, Toro, and Ankole had been in existence for hundreds of years.

During the late 1800s, the search for the headwaters of the Nile River drew many British explorers to East Africa. The first of these to reach Uganda was John Hanning Speke, who discovered Lake Victoria in 1858 and named it for the queen of England. Speke found the mouth of the Nile at this lake in 1862. Although he was certain of his discovery, no one could confirm his theory that the Nile originated in Lake Victoria until long after his death.

During Speke's exploration, he met with Mutesa I, the *kabaka* (king) of the Buganda tribe. Speke was astonished to see that the Buganda (or

Ganda) people were remarkably advanced for a supposedly primitive society. They lived in beautiful, five-story houses decorated with bones and shells. And the village men and women played sophisticated musical instruments similar to flutes, trumpets, and harps.

British Control

Speke's glowing accounts of the Ganda people encouraged British interest in the Uganda region. More explorers flocked to the area, followed by Christian missionaries. In 1888, a royal charter assigned control of the region to the Imperial British East Africa Company. Five years later, the company gave up the expense and difficulty of trying to oversee this inland area, and the British government took over the administration of the region.

In 1894, the British established the Buganda kingdom as a protectorate (dependent state), and soon they conquered the other tribes. The Ganda submitted to foreign control but still maintained their traditional way of life, and Britain took none of their land. Other tribes were upset with the special treatment shown the Ganda, but although kingdoms such as the Toro and Ankole received recognition, they were not allowed to keep their land.

The British saw Uganda's potential but recognized the problem of its remote location. To solve this problem, they began building the East African railroad to link Uganda's fertile interior to Kenya's ports. They wanted to transport Uganda's agricultural wealth to the port of Mombasa, and they also hoped to bring machinery and construction material inland for the development of the country. To lay the railroad track, Britain hired hundreds of Pakistani and Indian workers, many of whom eventually settled in Uganda. Construction was difficult; the workers had to labor through swamplands, thick forests, mountains, and the Great Rift Valley.

Many tribal rulers did not appreciate the British presence. Some reluctantly submitted to Britain's plans, but others led revolts. In 1897, Kabaka Mwanga, then the ruler of Buganda, attempted unsuccessfully to regain his kingdom's independence. The British replaced him with his young son, Daudi Chwa. Undaunted, Mwanga initiated three more revolts, each one unsuccessful. Finally, the British captured him and exiled him to a tiny group of islands in the Indian Ocean, where he died in 1903.

Although many of the tribes continued to resent the protectorate, the British did manage to bring some positive reforms to Uganda. They showed the people how to grow cotton and how to fashion garments, and a prosperous peasant economy later developed based on the cotton industry these reforms introduced. In addition, the British taught the people the value of their native coffee plants. Soon coffee production was a thriving industry.

Trying to maintain peace in the Buganda region, the British signed an agreement with the Ganda in 1900. Among other things, this document gave the tribe the right to retain a lawmaking body, comprised of a council of chiefs. The agreement also guaranteed that the land ownership system that had existed for hundreds of years could continue. The special privileges granted to the Ganda did not improve relations with other tribes. Another British move further increased friction within the country. When the East African railroad was completed, the British encouraged the Asians to develop the Ugandan economy, particularly its cotton and retail trades. As the Asians prospered, however, many native Ugandans began to resent their presence in the country. By the 1940s, anti-Asian riots had become common.

After many years as ruler of Buganda, Daudi Chwa died in 1939. His son, Edward Frederick Mutesa (nicknamed King Freddie), succeeded to the throne as Kabaka Mutesa II. For a time, Buganda continued as a protectorate within a country. The British, however, gradually became less willing to share their power, and after World War II ended in 1945, they attempted to establish a unified Ugandan nation. They saw Uganda's agricultural wealth as a way to revive their own dismal postwar economy.

During World War II, the British African colonies had become more independent, and this trend continued after the war. In 1948, the British

This old drawing shows Speke and another explorer at the court of King Mutesa I.

established the East African High Commission to coordinate agriculture, health, and telecommunications services in the three East African countries they ruled: Uganda, Kenya, and Tanganyika (now part of Tanzania). The Buganda greatly feared this interference, regarding it as the first step toward Britain's eventual takeover of Uganda. But other tribes disagreed and, jealous of Buganda's status as a protectorate, willfully sided with the British.

Government conditions became more complicated in the 1950s. Other British African colonies were developing nationalist movements and calling for independence. Britain continued to encourage efforts to establish a single unified nation in Uganda. Many of Uganda's tribal kingdoms pledged their support for this idea and organized a nationalist movement. Feeling threatened, the Ganda chiefs began to voice their concerns. In 1953, the British responded by deporting some of them, including the kabaka, to England, so they could not instigate a full-scale rebellion. The Ganda became extremely alarmed. To appease them, the British allowed the kabaka to return from his exile in 1955. In return, he promised to remain loyal to the British throne as long as Buganda was allowed to remain an independent nation.

Independence

By the end of the 1950s, the Ugandan nationalist movement had gained the support of most of the non-Ganda tribes, including the Acholi, Lango, Banyoro, and Bastoro. Finally, the Ganda kabaka reversed his former position and sided with the movement, maintaining that Buganda should be the administrative center for a new national government. *Uhuru* (independence) was declared on October 9, 1962. Mutesa II continued in his

Prime Minister Obote speaks to the people in 1965. A year later, he named himself president.

position as leader of Buganda, but the rest of Uganda elected as its prime minister Apollo Milton Obote, who was from the north—a region that had traditionally been hostile to the Buganda tribe.

In 1963, one year after independence, Uganda's Parliament elected Mutesa II the first president of Uganda. His power was extremely limited, however, and the prime minister retained control of the government. Although Prime Minister Obote's duty was to unify the country's warring peoples, his struggles with the Ganda became more and more heated. In 1966, Obote completely took over the new government and elected himself president. He then abolished the 1962 constitution, which had allowed Buganda to retain the rights of an independent state. Obote deported President Mutesa from the country, forbidding him ever to return to his homeland.

When Obote's new constitution went into effect in 1966, it greatly increased the president's powers. In fact, he now had all the power. In 1967, the government rewrote the constitution, asserting that it would dissolve all kingdoms and establish an official political party, the Uganda People's Congress. Most of its members were not of the Ganda tribe. The official government party considered its opponents to be criminals. The harsh policies of the new dictator only served to unite the people of Buganda in their opposition to him.

In 1969, Obote began to step up efforts to create a Socialist state in Uganda. Many people were upset by the left-wing turn of the government. Obote publicly declared his desire to make all businesses within the country the property of the state. He became increasingly power-hungry. In addition, he continued to show favoritism, particularly to members of the Lango tribe, of which he was a member, and to the Acholi people, many of whom served in his army.

Perhaps the most crucial event in modern Uganda's history occurred in January 1971, when the military overthrew the government in a coup d'etat. At the time of the coup, Obote was out of the country, attending a Commonwealth Prime Ministers' Conference in Singapore. The leader of the coup was Idi Amin, the commander of the army and a close friend of Obote. A member of the Kakwa tribe, Amin won support by courting the Ganda people, who had been disenchanted by the Obote government. The majority of Ugandans saw Amin as a strong leader who was genuinely concerned about the welfare of Uganda.

Although Amin declared that there would be no return to the tribal kingdoms, he pleased the Ganda by bringing back the body of Mutesa II from England, where he had died in exile in 1969, so that the kabaka could be buried in his homeland. He authorized an official state funeral for Mutesa II, burying him in the royal Kasubi Tombs on one of the seven hilltops of the capital city of Kampala.

Soon, Amin proclaimed that free and fair elections would resume. (No national election had been conducted in the country since 1962.) Obote had not returned to Uganda, and word spread that he was in hiding in Tanzania. People began to believe that the affairs of the country were looking up.

A Nation in Decline

The Ugandan people's hopefulness was short-lived, however. It soon became apparent that Amin was just as power-hungry as his predecessor had been. In March 1971, he signed the Suspension of Political Activities Decree. This took away many constitutional rights, such as freedom from arbitrary arrest and freedom of expression, assembly, association, and movement. Even worse, Amin gave the military vast powers to arrest citizens. His soldiers began to shoot on sight anyone they suspected of being a criminal. Many innocent people—including women and children—were killed.

After a while, many people began to have serious doubts about Amin's mental stability. He appeared to change his mind about issues from day to day. For example, he had originally supported Israel and had even brought many Israelis to Uganda to assist in the development of the new nation. But suddenly, in 1972, he showed extremely anti-Semitic behavior. He

Amin forced more than 73,000 Asians to leave Uganda in 1972—a move that crippled the economy.

decided to deport all Israeli business, military, and technical advisers. Some thought that Amin was trying to ally himself with the oil-rich Arab nations, especially Libya. Later, Amin acknowledged that Libya's Colonel Moammar Qaddafi was indeed giving financial aid to Uganda. Amin needed this money for his soaring military budget; the size of the military doubled in the 1970s.

Amin made public statements about his anti-Semitic feelings. In one telegram to the United Nations secretary general, he applauded Adolf Hitler's policy of genocide during World War II. In another, he praised the murders of the Israeli athletes during the 1972 Munich Olympics.

Amin made other troubling announcements during the summer of 1972. One was his decision that all Asians with British passports must leave Uganda within 90 days. Some saw this decision as Uganda's final rebellion against British colonialism. More than 50,000 people were affected by Amin's decree. A few weeks later, he expelled 23,000 additional Asians, most of whom were officially citizens of Uganda. Amin claimed his actions were part of his attempt to create the first black African state. However, many believed that Amin was jealous of the Asians, who had controlled the majority of the country's commerce and trade. Most of Uganda's doctors and teachers were also of Asian extraction. Although the Asians had comprised a mere 1 percent of the population, they were a powerful minority.

The Asian expulsion was designed to direct the people's attention away from the government's internal problems. The government took over the abandoned businesses, and Amin gave them to favored Ugandans. The long-term effects of this action were devastating. More than 80 percent of the shops in Kampala shut down. Schools closed because of a lack of available teachers. Industries suffered because there were no experienced managers left.

Amin further restricted civil rights in 1972. In the final months of that year, the first ethnic killings occurred, as the military began randomly murdering Lango and Acholi people, noted for their support of Obote. Intellectuals were systematically arrested, taken away in the night, and never heard from again. Among the missing people presumably murdered were a noted lawyer and politician, Benedicto Kiwanuka, and the archbishop of the Church of Uganda, Janani Luwum.

In June 1976, Uganda commanded world attention when a hijacked Air France jet landed at Entebbe airport near Kampala. The hijackers

In 1976, terrorists hijacked a jet and 100 hostages to Entebbe Airport near Kampala.

demanded the release of prisoners in Israel and other nations. The incident went on for a week. Some hostages were released after Amin bargained with the hijackers, but he failed to win the release of more than 100 Israeli passengers. Finally, an Israeli commando unit attacked the terrorists and freed the hostages. Three hostages were killed. Some people accused Amin of cooperating with the hijackers, saying the landing at Entebbe was preplanned and noting that four of the prisoners whose release the hijackers had demanded were Ugandans.

Great Britain severed diplomatic relations with Uganda after this incident. In 1977, Amnesty International estimated that Uganda's Military Intelligence Unit, Public Safety Unit, and Military Police had killed as many as 300,000 Ugandan citizens. The United States cut off trade with Uganda in 1978 because of such gross violations of human rights.

As Amin's regime continued, the country's lack of stable leadership became more evident. Roads crumbled. The economy was a shambles. Farmers were reduced to growing only enough food for their own use. Imports and exports dropped to dangerously low levels. Coffee remained in warehouses. Cotton, tea, and sugar were no longer harvested. Soon, Uganda's major trading partners began demanding payment for debts. Kenya, for example, refused to ship any more gasoline until Uganda paid its bills.

In October 1978, Amin staged a raid into the neighboring nation of Tanzania. He claimed his action was in retaliation for a Tanzanian attack, but Tanzania strongly denied attacking Uganda. Many people assumed the move was another of Amin's attempts to divert his people's attention from problems at home. His mission was unsuccessful. Tanzania's President Nyerere's forces defeated the Ugandan army; by April 1979, the Tanzanian army had advanced upon Kampala. Amid growing discontent among the Ugandan people, Idi Amin fled to Libya that month.

After Amin

Meanwhile, Ugandan exiles had formed a new political group in Tanzania. They called themselves the Ugandan National Liberation Front (UNLF). They were concerned about the threat of total anarchy in their former country and wanted to restore a peaceful government. Their meetings, however, were far from civil. Members were bitterly divided along regional and tribal lines. However, they managed to elect a leader, Yusufu Lule, a former head of Uganda's prestigious Makerere University, to rule Uganda. Lule promised free and fair popular elections, although he called for a ban on rival political parties.

Lule's time in office proved short. The other UNLF leaders found his attitude overbearing, and they forced him to resign in June 1979. To replace Lule they chose Godfrey Binaisa, known for his connections to former prime minister Obote. But Binaisa, too, proved to be a disappointment. When he conducted "free" elections, he did not permit certain political parties to run against him.

In May 1980, Obote returned from exile. Then a group of military officers overthrew Binaisa, accused him of government corruption, and held him in prison. Paulo Muwanga, the chairman of the military commission of the UNLF, reversed the ban on political parties.

Obote unofficially took over as president. He still had sizable support from certain quarters, although most people could not forget the corruption of his last administration and did not welcome his return. Although some Ugandans remained wary, others flocked back to the country from exile. Many of these, however, became terribly disheartened upon their return. They had hoped to find a peaceful Uganda, but the situation was worse than it ever had been. Mobs looted stores and murdered innocent people in the streets. Rioters severely damaged many cities and villages, some of which have yet to recover. Fighting and vandalism made a shambles of Kampala. The army was divided, and there was no longer any police force to control the situation. It appeared that law and order would never be restored.

To make matters worse, northeastern Uganda suffered a severe famine during this time, and the government provided no aid. An estimated 30,000 people died. Foreign relief organizations attempted to help but had difficulty making arrangements with the government.

In October 1980, the Obote government claimed that a group of Amin supporters had invaded the western provinces of Uganda. Obote ordered a revenge attack on the West Nile Province, Amin's homeland. As a result, 250,000 people were reportedly displaced.

In December 1980, Uganda held its first general election since April 1962. Rival political parties contested the results, alleging that polling hours had been extended in certain regions, but appointed observers contended that the elections were valid. On December 15, Obote was declared the official president of Uganda. He immediately increased the size of his

Parliament, filling its ranks with those who shared his political viewpoint. Many supporters of the opposition left the country, realizing that the oppressive new government would not tolerate their views.

Problems worsened through the early 1980s. Some people, no longer able to contend with the Obote government, took their cause to the streets. Tolerating no opposition, Obote sent armed troops to patrol the villages and towns. Anyone suspected of being a member of the opposition

President Obote's administration was a violent and repressive military dictatorship.

was thrown in jail. Uganda became notorious for its inhumane, over-crowded prisons. Inmates were beaten, tortured, and starved.

Obote outlawed the opposition press and ordered many newspapers and radio stations to shut down. A guerrilla movement led by Yoweri Museveni, called the National Resistance Army, got a foothold and launched a series of attacks against Obote. Other groups worked feverishly to depose the government. During the early 1980s, attacks on military

Ugandan president Yoweri Museveni arrives in Nairobi on a four-day state visit to Kenya to discuss greater East African cooperation.

posts and police stations were commonplace as terrorism reached new heights in Kampala.

Museveni initially centered his military operations in the Luwero district, a region of rich and fertile farmlands that was an important agricultural center. During Obote's presidency, the Luwero lost most of its estimated 750,000 residents. Although the whereabouts of some of these people are still unknown, the U.S. State Department believes that Obote's troops murdered nearly 500,000 of them. During the worst of the struggle, Obote's soldiers simply rounded up the villagers in the region, labeled them antigovernment guerrillas, and shot them. No one was safe from the secret police—not even women or children.

The resistance continued for several years. Finally, in July 1985, Tito Okello, an army commander, ousted Obote. On January 26, 1986, Yoweri Museveni took control of the government. Museveni had already won the respect of some people because his troops did not slaughter citizens as had other leaders' soldiers.

Museveni promised he would rule for four years. In 1989, however, his government extended its rule for five more years. At last, on October 8, 1995, a new constitution went into effect, and seven months later, on May 9, 1996, Uganda held its first election under the new constitution. Museveni was elected president with 74 percent of the vote. On June 27, 1996, a new National Assembly was elected as well. The Assembly had 276 members—214 of them directly elected by the voters in their districts.

Several foreign governments expressed criticisms of the electoral process. Museveni faced two opposition candidates during the campaign, but he had advantages his opponents didn't have. He received the uncritical support of the government-owned daily newspaper, for example, and he controlled a $3 million presidential fund he could use to reward supporters.

On the other hand, Museveni has given his country its first period of stable, peaceful government. His economic policies have helped bring Uganda the fastest economic growth rate in Africa. He has also re-established the court system, increased freedom of the press, and encouraged the return of the Asian and British exiles.

The people of Uganda belong to about 40 tribal groups. Over 80 percent of the people are agricultural workers, including this man.

Uganda's People

The people of Uganda present a colorful and diverse picture. The majority of the population is of black African ancestry, descending from about 40 tribes. Of these, the Buganda tribe is the largest. Other major tribes include the Iteso, Ankole, and Basoga. Most non-African Ugandans are descendants of Indians and Pakistanis, whose ancestors were brought to Uganda to work on the East African railway in the early 1900s.

Before the early 1970s, many British people resided in Uganda. Descendants of the British settlers who began arriving in Uganda in the late 1800s, they lived in and around the major cities, particularly Kampala. Like the Asians, they were heavily involved in commerce and industry, operating farms, plantations, stores, and farms. Others worked as doctors, teachers, and lawyers. Idi Amin deported nearly all of them during his reign.

Although few Britons remain in Uganda, they have left their mark on the country. They introduced the English language to Uganda, and today it is Uganda's official language. Many people speak it as a second language, and most attempt to learn it because it helps them in the job market. Many people, especially those in the military, also speak Swahili, which is considered to be the national language. In addition, many tribes have their own dialects.

Tribal Traditions

The concept of the extended family is a universal Ugandan tradition. Each Ugandan man is responsible for his entire family, including cousins, uncles, and even distant relations. (A husband never considers his wife to be part of his family. Instead, he regards her as her father's daughter.) This responsibility can be quite taxing. Not only must a man open his home to his relatives, but he must also care for them when they are ill. He must help them rebuild their houses if they are destroyed or damaged. And if he becomes wealthy, he must share his wealth with them.

In recent years, many young people have shirked their duties to the extended family. They feel that family responsibilities have prevented them from moving up in society. Often, after their duties to the extended family are fulfilled, they have no money for themselves. Sometimes young people feel compelled to make a complete break with their families. Still, most Ugandans rely on their relatives and expect their relatives to rely on them.

Other traditions remain as well. For example, a boy must undergo an initiation rite to prove he is strong enough to enter the adult world. Sometimes he is required to perform a special task. In other instances, he receives a mark on his skin proving he is a member of a tribe.

Most boys and girls marry when they are still in their teens. Although romantic marriages for love are common in Uganda, the parents of the intended couple must approve the marriage. When a boy wants to marry a girl, he must give her parents a set of gifts, commonly known as bridewealth. Typical bridewealth gifts include goats, cattle, and chickens. Lately, the gifts have become more contemporary, sometimes including Western shirts, dresses, furniture, and televisions. Sometimes a husband will take his gifts back if his wife does not become pregnant. The transfer of gifts is considered more important than the ceremony, and the bride's parents will be very angry if the groom cannot afford his bridewealth. When this happens, some couples elope.

Divorce is common in Uganda, although it is sometimes easier for a man to take another wife than to go through the divorce process. There

(continued on page 57)

SCENES OF
UGANDA

➤ *Monkeys and baboons thrive in the rural regions.*

◄ *Although they cannot fly, ostriches can run across the savanna at high speeds.*

▲ *The white rhinoceros lives near rivers and lakes throughout much of East Africa.*

◄ *The tiny dik-dik is a native species of antelope.*

◄ This man of the Madi tribe wears a traditional feathered headdress and a leopard skin.

➤ Native kings, or kabakas, were buried in special royal tombs like this one in Kampala.

⋏ *The hardy baobab tree is one of the most common sights on the hot, dry plains.*

➤ *Downtown Kampala is a showcase of modern buildings, wide streets, and lush gardens.*

∨ *Queen Elizabeth Park is a typical Ugandan landscape of mountains, lake, and forest.*

➤ Ugandans can step
from one hemisphere
to the other.

➤ *Volcanic soil supports varied and luxuriant plant life.*

⋎ *Flowering jacaranda trees soften a view of the distant Ruwenzori Mountains.*

(continued from page 48)

are still areas where tribesmen have more than one wife. The tribespeople defend multiple marriages, saying there is a shortage of available men in Uganda. A woman who shares her husband with other wives rarely lives with him. More likely, she lives with her children in a hut on the outskirts of the village, and her husband provides her with food and supplies. Most Ugandan women are completely dependent on their husbands, because they receive no income or inheritance. Money is usually passed from father to son.

Rural Life

Most villagers are self-employed farmers. The typical village is surrounded by banana trees and sweeping fields of peanuts, cassava, millet, and maize. Traditionally, men do the heavy work on the farms. Women sometimes help with the planting and weeding, but spend most of their time caring for the children and preparing meals. Villagers do most of their field work before noon, when they return to their huts to escape the oppressive sun.

The typical village residence is simply constructed, with a roof made of dry palm leaves or elephant grass and walls of red clay, supported by the branches of sturdy trees. Sometimes neighboring huts are attached, with several families living under a single roof. Occasionally, Ugandans build houses with tin roofs and cinderblock walls.

Religious Life

Religion plays an important role in the lives of Uganda's people. Although religious groups suffered persecution under the Amin and Obote regimes, Christianity, Islam, and tribal religions continue to flourish.

Most Ugandans practice a Christian religion. About 33 percent are Roman Catholic. Although the Catholic church founded missions there in the late 1800s, Uganda did not choose its first bishop until 1953, when the country was divided into separate dioceses. Today, Uganda has 15 Catholic dioceses, many of which are led by native Ugandan bishops. Other bishops are foreigners from Europe or adjacent countries.

About 33 percent of Ugandans are Protestant. Many of these belong to the Church of Uganda. Others belong to the Anglican church, the Pentecostal Assembly of God, or the Baptist Church of Uganda.

Muslims comprise 16 percent of the population. After the 1972 Asian deportation, Idi Amin converted to Islam. He authorized the con-

Family ties and responsibilities are a big part of life, according to tribal traditions.

struction of an Islamic university, but it was never built and the funds he received for it were channeled elsewhere.

Some tribes still follow their traditional religions. These groups include the Dodoth, the Jie, and the Karamojong, all of which live in the northeastern sections of the country. And many of the people who practice an organized religion retain some tribal beliefs.

Most of Uganda's 40 tribes retain some traditional religious beliefs. Many of these are concerned with the supernatural world—especially with the relationship between the world of the living and the world of the dead. Followers often believe in several gods: a high god and a collection of lesser spirits.

Some tribespeople believe in the ancestral cult, which holds that dead ancestors have the power to shape everyday lives. For example, when a believer runs into bad luck, he assumes that his ancestors are angry with him. He tries to win back their favor by changing his lifestyle or by offering them gifts of food and drink. He promises to stop any behavior that offends them. Cultists believe that their ancestors want them to uphold tribal traditions. While they invest ultimate power in the high god, they consider him somewhat remote from their everyday lives, so they pray to their ancestors when they seek advice about marriages, traveling, or raising children. Sometimes people will consult a diviner—a person who they believe has the power to contact the world of the dead—to assist them in their efforts to reach their ancestors.

The tribal ritual is another important part of many tribal faiths. Basically, a tribal ritual is a ceremony for the living to communicate with supernatural forces. Many Ugandans—even those who practice other religions—regard this ritual as the surest way to maintain a good relationship with the higher powers. Sometimes tribespeople conduct a ritual to ask for help. At other times, they do so to express praise and thanksgiving.

Although one person may conduct a ritual, more often several people are involved. The inauguration of a new tribal chief is one occasion for such a ritual. During the ceremony, people dance, sing, and play musical instruments. They eat foods prepared especially for the occasion. Some wear flamboyant, colorful robes.

Other occasions for rituals include the onset of puberty (the initiation rite), birth, marriage, and death. Sometimes people gather to ask the higher forces to end a drought. They regularly hold rituals on the first day of the planting season, as well as after the harvest.

A parade gathers on October 9, 1962, the country's first Independence Day.

In addition to religious observances and tribal ceremonies, Ugandans celebrate a number of national holidays. The official holidays include New Year's Day, Liberation Day (January 26), International Woman's Day (March 8), Labor Day (May 1), Martyr's Day (June 3), National Heroes Day (June 9), and Independence Day (October 9). Uganda also recognizes both Christian and Muslim holidays.

Cultural Life

Art plays an important part in everyday life in Uganda. Over the past few decades, the government has begun to encourage people to preserve their cultures, and it has established museums in Kampala to display Ugandan handicrafts, clothing, and pottery.

People throughout the world have begun to recognize the value of Uganda's tribal art forms. Many museums display Ugandan ceremonial masks, ebony statues, and ornaments covered with gold leaf. Ugandan statues receive the most attention. Art experts can usually identify the creator's tribe by the statue's design, because each tribe has formulated its own principles of workmanship. While some statues display details that are almost realistic, others have distorted limbs and features. Ugandans often use the distorted statues in religious ceremonies to chase away evil spirits.

Music and Dance

Other art forms also play a role in tribal life. Music and dance are important features of tribal rituals. During a celebration, participants play drums, gongs, rattles, and wind and string instruments. The tribal dances are rooted in drum rhythms, and drummers play a particular rhythm for each occasion. The drums themselves are intriguing examples of design. Most often, they are made from a hollow log with a slit on the side. The pitch and tone depend upon the size of this slit. For a different effect, artisans cover it with an elephant's ear.

Anthropologists once believed that tribespeople used the drums to scare evil spirits. Now they know that the drums transmit messages from tribe to tribe. Sometimes a message completes a 100-mile (160-kilometer) journey in less than an hour.

The Uganda Museum in Kampala features musical instruments, which the attendants will play for visitors, as well as other tribal artwork. The National Theater and Cultural Center, also in Kampala, supports native music, theater, and dance. It presents programs locally and also sends its troupes, including a well-known dance company, to other countries.

A woman of Masooli wears the busuti *dress introduced by Victorian missionaries.*

Costumes and Clothing

Ceremonial costumes also reflect the talents of the tribal artisans. These outfits are intricately decorated with bones, animal horns, hides, shells, and feathers. Some of the participants wear elaborate headdresses decorated with ostrich feathers, or attach strands of giraffe hair to the back of their heads.

When not taking part in a tribal ceremony, many rural women, especially those living in the eastern sections of the country, wear the traditional Ugandan costume called the *busuti*. Introduced by missionaries in the 1870s, the busuti resembles a Victorian-style dress. It has a square neckline, short sleeves, and a long, flowing skirt with a swatch of cloth running diagonally from the waist to the hip. Typically, a woman uses 7 yards (6.4 meters) of material to make a busuti, dying the material a variety of colors such as peach, lavender, and pale yellow.

Another traditional Ugandan fabric is the *kanga* cloth. Manufactured in Jinja's textile mills, a piece of kanga cloth is usually 10 feet (3 meters) long and 3 feet (.9 m) wide and often is printed with African proverbs. Because it is so inexpensive, women buy it in large quantities and fashion many outfits from it.

Unlike Ugandan women, most Ugandan men dress in Western-style clothes. But in remote areas of the country, some men still wear the *kanzu*, a long garment that resembles a nightshirt. Occasionally, Muslim men dress in long, flowing robes.

Food and Drink

Traditional Ugandan foods mostly consist of the grains, fruits, and vegetables that grow in abundance. *Posho* is a porridge made from maize flour and water. Sometimes millet and cassava are added to the mixture. In areas where bananas are plentiful, *matoke* is a popular dish. Matoke is prepared by mashing bananas into a pulp that is then shaped into little balls, wrapped in banana leaves, and steamed. It is usually served with other foods, including fish, meat, and ground peanuts. Roasted sweet potatoes and broiled cassava are popular dishes, and peanuts are sometimes used to make soup stock. Ugandans make beer from maize, millet, sorghum, sugarcane, and bananas. Although it is illegal to make homemade alcoholic beverages, the law is rarely enforced.

During the early 1900s, Ugandans developed a taste for foods introduced by the foreigners in the country. *Samosa*, first introduced by the Indians, is a highly-seasoned pastry filled with steamed vegetables. Ugandans also enjoy British favorites, including Yorkshire pudding, custard sauce, and treacle. British-style pubs and restaurants can be found throughout Kampala.

Recreation

Uganda is a sports-lover's paradise. Many people participate in organized sports introduced by the British, including hockey, rugby, cricket, tennis, squash, and netball. The most popular sport is British-style football (known as soccer in the United States). Ugandans flock to the games every week. Championships are held once a year in Kampala.

Fishing is another popular sport. Freshwater varieties, such as perch, tiger fish, lungfish, and catfish, abound in Lake Albert and in the Nile between the Sudan border and Murchison Falls. Rainbow trout thrive in the Mount Elgon region. In certain isolated locations, giant catfish and electric eels swim.

Mountain climbing and canoe racing are also favorite pastimes. Ugandan teenagers learn climbing skills and master the most challenging peaks. The mountain club of Uganda takes experienced climbers on regular expeditions to the Ruwenzori. On special occasions, Ugandans race canoes on Lake Victoria. This is also a popular spectator sport.

The Parliament Building, located in Kampala, is the home of the 276-member National Assembly.

Government

Like many African countries, Uganda is in transition, searching for a form of government that meshes with its own unique social systems. Although many Ugandans hoped independence would lead them to self-sufficiency, they soon realized that this process would not happen overnight.

In the years since independence, Uganda has had a series of constitutions, but the country's leaders have rarely upheld them. Both Milton Obote and Idi Amin adapted the government to suit themselves. During their years in power, the structure of both local and national government dissolved as leaders were appointed or dismissed at whim.

Currently, under the constitution adopted in 1995, the president is directly elected by the people of Uganda. The legislative branch of the government, the National Assembly, has 276 members. Of these, 214 members are elected in single-seat constituencies, in the same way senators and congresspersons are elected in the United States. Thirty-nine seats are reserved for "indirectly elected" women; similarly, 10 seats are set aside for the army, 5 for people with disabilities, 5 for youth, and 3 for trade unions.

Many political complications have come from the way Britain treated Uganda's tribal kingdoms during the protectorate. When Britain established the boundary lines for the districts, some rival tribes found themselves in the same districts. In addition, some of the kingdoms have had hostile relationships with the central government. Buganda, for instance, was reluctant to give up its autonomy after independence. Although the Museveni government has said that individual tribes are not as important as a united Uganda, many of the tribespeople have found this hard to accept.

Museveni believes that political parties encourage ethnic and regional divisions. He has argued that Uganda needs a "no-party" system, rather than the multiparty system found in most modern democracies. Under the 1995 constitution, all political candidates must run as individuals, without party labels.

The ban on parties may be lifted in the near future, however. Under the constitution, Uganda is supposed to hold a national referendum after the current system has been put through a trial period. If the people vote in favor of parties, Uganda will become a multiparty state. In the meantime, parties can exist, but they cannot sponsor candidates in elections.

The judicial system consists of magistrate's courts, a High Court with 21 judges, and a Supreme Court. The High Court has full jurisdiction over criminal and civil cases in the entire country. The magistrate's courts are lower-ranking courts with a more limited jurisdiction. The Supreme Court hears appeals from the High Court, and the High Court hears appeals from the magistrate's courts.

Health Care

Health care was a priority during the 1960s, when clinics opened in the villages and countryside, and the government devoted almost 10 percent of its budget to health expenditures. Many villagers attended classes in nutrition. The government established vaccination programs to prevent small-pox, measles, tuberculosis, and other serious diseases. It also instituted projects to control malaria-carrying mosquitos.

The early Obote administration also made a concentrated effort to open as many hospitals as possible, building more than 22 in a ten-year period. The most famous of these hospitals, Mulago in Kampala, was one of the finest on the African continent. However, by the early 1980s, the budget for health care had fallen to less than 3 percent of the total. It reached 9.9 percent in 1990, under the Museveni government, but fell again to 3.9 percent by the mid-1990s. Life expectancy in Uganda is only 40 years, terribly low for a nation that once had a sophisticated health system. The infant mortality rate is 99.4 deaths per 1,000 births.

Health problems in Uganda are especially severe in the rural areas, where leprosy and polio are widespread. Many villagers still believe illness to be a curse and seek treatment from witch doctors or medicine men.

Poor nutrition aggravates Uganda's health problems. Some Ugandan children suffer from *kwashiorkor*, a disease caused by lack of protein in the diet that produces swelling in the arms, legs, and stomach and alters pigmentation of the skin and hair. Doctors encourage parents to supplement their children's mostly carbohydrate diets with protein-rich foods such as peanuts, fish, beans, and termites.

In addition to poor nutrition, many Ugandans suffer from malaria, schistosomiasis, and sleeping sickness. Malaria, a disease passed to humans by means of a bite from a malaria-carrying mosquito, causes high fevers, sweating, and convulsions. Schistosomiasis is spread by freshwater flukes, which penetrate the skin and enter the bloodstream. Although much research has been conducted on ways to prevent this disease, there is still no known cure. Sleeping sickness can now be cured, but its primary means of transmission, the tsetse fly, still infests certain areas.

Many doctors fled the country during the struggle between Obote and Museveni's resistance movement. Many hospitals were virtually destroyed. At one time, Nakaseke Hospital was one of Africa's better-equipped rural hospitals. It even provided both dental care and outpatient services. Nearly 100 professionals served on its staff. But Obote's army made no attempt to steer clear of Nakaseke when it launched attacks in the nearby regions. It cleared out the hospital complex—even stripping away the padding on the last operating table. The military harassed and attacked hospital employees and placed patients under arrest, sometimes even carrying them away in the midst of surgery. Obote's forces also took away doctors suspected of helping the guerrillas.

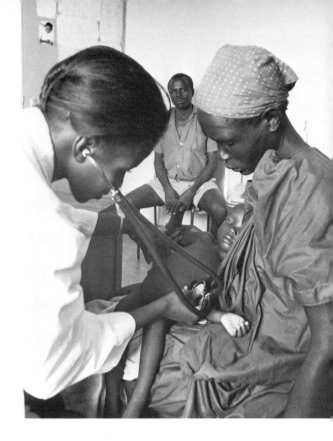

*This child suffers from
malnutrition, one of
Uganda's most serious
health problems.*

As a result of such turmoil, Uganda today has about one doctor for every 25,000 people. In wealthy countries such as the United States, the average is one doctor for every 390 people.

In addition to all its other health problems, Uganda has one of the highest rates of acquired immunodeficiency syndrome (AIDS) in the world. According to the World Health Organization, over 14 percent of the adult population may be infected with HIV, the virus that causes AIDS. A British medical study found that 41 percent of all the adult deaths in one rural area were caused by AIDS. The government is fighting back with an educational program aimed at reducing the sexual transmission of the virus, and recent studies show that the program is having an effect.

Education

Uganda has an educational tradition that dates back hundreds of years. In the tribal era, the villages would choose the brightest young men and send them to study with the higher chiefs. The country has many mission schools that were established in the Victorian era. In 1875, the Church Missionary Society sent its first missionaries to the region. Alexander Mackay, the son of a Scottish minister, was one of the first to arrive. He set up a makeshift printing press and printed prayer books, hymnals, and textbooks for prospective students. Later, Kabaka Mutesa I invited missionaries to teach the most gifted children of the Buganda tribe.

By 1970, more than 120,000 students were enrolled in Roman Catholic and Anglican schools throughout Uganda. Public education was also on the upswing. When Uganda became an independent country, the government established a national public school system. As part of his cabinet, the president set up a minister of education, who was responsible for developing educational programs as well as promoting literacy among adults. Before the 1971 rebellion, Uganda spent more than 25 percent of its annual budget on educational programs. In the 1960s, the government hoped that one in every four Ugandan children would complete high school and that some of those children would go on to college. But education has suffered since that time because of Uganda's internal problems. The country is still attempting to reach its educational goals. Today, 62 percent of adults can read and write.

For most of the nation's history, there was no free education in Uganda. Students paid fees from the day they started primary school. In 1997, however, the government launched a program called Universal Primary Education (UPE). At present, the program provides free primary education for four children per family. Eventually, it is supposed to provide free primary education for all children.

Under the Ugandan system, seven years of primary school are followed by four years of high school. Students who finish the four-year program receive an Ordinary Level high school certificate. If they complete two more years, they receive an Advanced Level Higher Education certificate.

Boys get a larger share of the country's educational resources—a common problem in poor countries. About 45 percent of the children enrolled in primary schools are girls. In the secondary schools, only 35 percent of the students are female.

The most promising students can continue their education at colleges and universities. Some of them leave Uganda for schools in Western Europe and the United States, and others attend Makerere University—one of Africa's most prestigious colleges. Located in Kampala, Makerere University began as a technical school in 1922 and became a full-fledged university in 1947. Students from all over the African continent are enrolled in full-time study there.

Makerere's beautifully landscaped campus is situated on a grassy knoll overlooking Kampala. The school has survived—and actually managed to grow—in spite of the damage inflicted on it by years of political turmoil. The worst incident occurred in 1976, during the Amin regime, when the military reportedly massacred 100 students. In addition, troops severely

Students study microscopic samples in the biology laboratory of Makerere University.

vandalized the school library, once the largest in all of East Africa, and carted away and burned many books.

Today, 7,000 students attend Makerere. Seventeen divisions offer degrees in law, science, engineering, the liberal arts, and most of the other subjects taught at leading universities. The School of Medicine is located at New Mulaga Hospital on Mulaga Hill, next to the main university campus. Like most schools of medicine, it is a research center. Students and faculty are working to rid the entire East African region of the parasites and jungle fevers that have hindered development there.

Extensive adult education programs are available throughout the country. Adults can attend classes in community centers and high school buildings to learn basic skills. They may also attend vocational classes to learn a particular trade, such as auto mechanics or farming, or to learn how to run a small business.

During the 1970s, the Ugandan government, with the help of experts from the United Nations, started livestock-breeding programs to create a beef industry.

Resources and Economy

Agriculture employs over 80 percent of Uganda's population. Thus, the economic welfare of the people depends largely upon Uganda's consistently good weather. The country rarely has to contend with drought and famine because of its high elevation and its rich volcanic soil, but insect infestation is sometimes a problem.

The Ugandans have largely neglected their country's other natural resources, such as minerals, petroleum, and other raw materials. Mineral deposits are often difficult and expensive to reach because they are situated in isolated, rural areas. Uganda's natural resources could become the basis of a thriving economy, but progress has been hindered by the country's political troubles and the poor condition of the transportation system.

Copper, Uganda's most plentiful resource, runs through the Kilembe mine in western Uganda, and some companies have managed to conduct mining operations there. But between 1970 and 1977, production dropped more than 85 percent and the mine closed.

Iron-ore deposits are plentiful enough to support a steel industry, but iron-ore mining seems unlikely until transportation methods improve. Other natural resources in Uganda include phosphates, sulfur, and salt. There are large salt deposits in and around the Lake Katwe region, and phosphate deposits run through the eastern region of the country. Limestone is abundant throughout Uganda, particularly near the eastern and western borders.

Aside from these major mineral deposits, several other minerals exist in smaller quantities in Uganda. These include beryllium, mica, gold, lead, tin, and tungsten. In the late 1990s, gold provided Uganda with almost 7 percent of the money it earned from exports.

Economy

In May 1987, President Museveni reached agreements for financial support from the International Monetary Fund and the World Bank. He committed Uganda to a market-oriented economic strategy. The program included measures such as currency reform, elimination of wage and price controls, and the privatization of enterprises that had been run by the state. In May

This plantation worker is picking tea, one of the country's four main cash crops. The others are coffee, cotton, and maize.

1991, Museveni formally invited the Asian exiles to return and promised their property would be given back to them.

These measures, and others designed to reduce the economic upheavals of earlier years, have paid off. Between 1987 and 1996, Uganda's economy grew at a rate that averaged about 7 percent a year. In the late 1990s, the annual growth rate sometimes passed 9 percent. In some sections of the economy, the growth rates were even higher. The manufacturing growth rate averaged 12.5 percent during the first ten years of the Museveni era.

Today, the major cash crops (those sold for profit) include coffee, cotton, tea, and maize (corn). There was a time when coffee and cotton accounted for 80 percent of all exports. But coffee production was particularly hard-hit during the Amin years, declining 25 percent between 1969 and 1978. World coffee prices fell in 1977, contributing to the problem. The demand for coffee began to rise by the early 1980s, and today coffee accounts for about 63 percent of all Ugandan exports.

The cotton industry suffered as well during the Amin regime. Today cotton provides about 2.3 percent of the country's export income. Tea and maize each provide about 2.6 percent. The 1972 deportations of Asians and British particularly hurt the tea and sugar industries, because these groups owned and managed many of the plantations.

Tourism is beginning to play a major role in Uganda's economy. In 1983, only 12,786 tourists visited the country. By the late 1990s, the count had passed the 175,000 mark. Uganda has beautiful scenery and a pleasant climate. Its national parks are a major attraction for tourists. Visitors to Mgahinga Gorilla National Park can see the world's largest primates in their own domain.

Despite the economic advances of recent years, Uganda is still one of the poorest nations in the world. Economists measure economies with a yardstick they call the gross domestic product (GDP)—the total value of all the goods and services produced in a country. Uganda's GDP per person is only $900. In the United States, in comparison, GDP per person is about

$27,500. But Uganda is finally starting to experience the kind of economic growth most poor countries want to achieve.

For rural Ugandans, talk about GDP and market strategies may seem irrelevant. Most people in Uganda's countryside purchase few luxury goods. Many of them build their own houses and live simple lives. Self-sufficient, they haul their water from the village well and cut down trees to provide fuel for cooking. Their few living expenses include school tuition and taxes, and sometimes special farming tools and equipment.

Kampala's busy bus station is typical of life in the fast-growing, lively capital city. Not only the seat of government, it is the country's commercial and cultural center as well.

City Life

Kampala is the capital of Uganda, with a population of more than 770,000. At an elevation of 4,000 feet (1,200 meters), Kampala enjoys a pleasant, mild climate. Only 4 miles (6.4 kilometers) from the shore of Lake Victoria, it serves as Uganda's chief commercial center. The city also has a major agricultural and livestock market.

Kampala was not established as a formal municipality until 1949. Much of its growth has been rather recent. Because most of the city is new, modern principles of city planning were incorporated into its design. All industrial areas of the city were located on the outskirts of town, away from residential areas. Within the city, roads radiate from the center like the spokes of a wheel, leading to rural areas of the country. Now that Uganda has become more stable, Kampala has once again become the showplace of the nation. The main shopping center along Kampala Road has been repaired. North of Kampala Road, there is a smart-looking area that houses government buildings, foreign embassies, and modern hotels. South of Kampala Road, however, lies an overcrowded slum.

Jinja is the second largest city in the country, with 45,000 residents. Located at the source of the Nile River, Jinja is about 50 miles (80 kilometers) east of the capital along the major railroad. Like Kampala, much of Jinja has developed recently.

Many of these bananas grown near the Ruwenzori foothills will be sent to city markets.

The development of Jinja began with the construction of the Owen Falls Dam in 1954. This government-owned dam provides hydroelectric power to numerous industrial facilities and provides most of the country's electricity. Many companies have established operations in Jinja, including plywood factories, copper smelters, steel and textile mills, and a tobacco factory.

Another important town is Entebbe, which was the capital of the country until 1962. Situated on Lake Victoria just north of the equator, Entebbe is the site of Uganda's major international airport. Because the city is only 21 miles (33 kilometers) from Kampala, it is sometimes regarded as a suburb rather than as a separate city.

Before the 1970s, many urban residents were Europeans and Asians who owned shops and managed businesses. Many of their homes fell into disrepair after they were exiled. Now that they have started returning, refurbished properties have become a common sight in the cities, especially in Kampala.

During the 1960s, experts from the United Nations and a variety of countries trained Ugandans in technical skills.

Transportation and Communications

Any country that is serious about developing its economy must maintain a good transportation system, so that manufactured goods will be able to reach the marketplace. Railways are the most reliable form of commercial transportation in Uganda. Consisting of about 770 miles (1,240 kilometers) of track, Uganda's railroad system connects the neighboring countries of Kenya and Tanzania. There are two separate branches within Uganda. One crosses the southwestern section near Kasase, and the other crosses the northwestern section near Lake Albert. The main spur leads to the Kenyan port of Mombasa, on the Indian Ocean.

Kenya, Tanzania, and Uganda shared ownership of the East African railway in the 1960s, but this partnership later dissolved and the three countries attempted to divide the assets evenly. After the breakup, many foreign countries, including India, France, and West Germany, bought stock in the Uganda Railway Corporation.

While Uganda's railway system has always been fairly successful, the road system has suffered from a number of problems, such as potholes that have made travel dangerous on many highways. Of the almost 19,000 miles (30,300 kilometers) of roads in Uganda, only 2,160 miles (3,480 kilometers) are paved and can be used year-round. In the mid-1980s, the country embarked on a major program to rebuild its roads. By the late

1990s, about 60 percent of the main roads had been rehabilitated, and the government was planning to invest approximately $1.5 billion in a new ten-year rebuilding project. Although many Ugandans own automobiles, road transportation consists primarily of buses, trucks, and jeeps.

Steamboats on Lake Victoria provide a valuable service to all of East Africa. They collect raw cotton at various towns along the lake and transport it to the mills of Jinja. They also pick up other raw materials, such as ores, along the shoreline and bring them to the town of Kisumu. From this point, the goods travel to the railroad, which carries them to Kenya.

Within the last few decades, air travel has become a major form of transportation in Uganda. Jumbo jets fly into and out of the country's international airport at Entebbe, 21 miles (33 kilometers) south of Kampala.

Communications

Uganda had a free press after independence, but Idi Amin banned many newspapers during his reign. Museveni has restored most press freedoms, and four daily newspapers are now published in Kampala. *The New Vision*, the official government paper, has a circulation of 30,000. The other dailies

Radio Uganda broadcasts in English, Swahili, and a number of tribal languages.

are *The Monitor* (30,000), *The Star* (5,000), and *Taifa Uganda Empya*, which is published in the Luganda language and has a circulation of 24,000.

Periodical publications include a Roman Catholic monthly, *Musizi*, which has a circulation of 30,000, and a Roman Catholic bi-monthly, *Leadership*, which reaches 7,400 readers. Other periodicals include *The Pearl of Africa*, an official government monthly; *The Exposure*, a political monthly; *Uganda Confidential* (monthly); and the *Eastern Africa Journal of Rural Development*, which appears twice a year. Several book publishers also operate in Uganda. Fountain Publishers produces textbooks, children's books, and academic and trade books. Centenary Publishing House Ltd. is an Anglican publishing house.

Radio and television are important means of communication within Uganda. By the mid-1990s, there were more than 2,210,000 radio receivers in the country. Radio Uganda broadcasts in English, Swahili, and 22 other languages. Television, too, experienced rapid growth in the 1990s. By the middle of the decade, there were approximately 230,000 sets in use in Uganda. Uganda Television Service is a government-controlled commercial service that currently transmits over a radius of 200 miles (320 kilometers) from Kampala. Most of the programs are in English, but the Television Service also broadcasts in Swahili and Luganda.

Although most Ugandan towns have telephone service, the quality is poor. The most modern equipment is located in Kampala. Outside the capital, the equipment tends to be older and is often in poor condition.

Uganda's farmers are replanting lands once devastated by civil conflict. If it can benefit from its fertile soil and hardworking people, Uganda may continue its progress.

Uganda:
Past and Present

The small country of Uganda is one of Africa's most beautiful lands. Mountains, grasslands, and arid plains provide sharply contrasting terrain. Several lakes and rivers, including Lake Victoria and the mighty Nile River, water the fertile soil. Many species of wild animals roam Uganda's national parks. The country has a moderate climate favorable to an agricultural economy.

Forty tribes, each with a different culture, inhabit Uganda. Tribal cultures and traditions are still very much in evidence in the rural regions, where most of the 20,100,000 residents live. Since the 1970s, many native Ugandans have come to live and work in the country's urban centers, such as Jinja, Entebbe, and Kampala, the capital city. However, many of these city residents still commute to and from rural villages each weekend.

Uganda has had a troubled history, marked by tribal rivalries, foreign oppression, and dictatorships. The former British protectorate gained its independence from Great Britain in 1962. For most of the next 25 years, it was poorly governed, abused by regimes interested not in the economic growth of the country but in the acquisition of power. Its first years as an independent nation were marked by social disintegration and economic decline.

Today, Uganda is finally beginning to make progress. Under the leadership of a government headed by a former guerrilla leader, Yoweri Museveni, Ugandans have achieved one of the highest economic growth rates in Africa. Uganda now has a chance to remedy the troubles that have plagued it and to regain its reputation as a beautiful land enhanced by rich cultural diversity.

◄ G L O S S A R Y ►

Ancestor cult	A group of tribespeople who worship the spirits of their dead ancestors. Cultists believe that their ancestors watch and influence the events of their daily lives, and offer prayers or sacrifices to them.
Busuti	The traditional costume of Ugandan women, with sleeves and a long, full skirt. Similar in style to the dresses of Victorian England, it was introduced by missionaries in the 1870s.
Cassava	A tropical plant grown for its fleshy, edible roots, which yield a nutritious starch. The cassava is typically ground into flour and prepared in breads, porridges, puddings, and fried cakes.
Coup d'etat	A French phrase, literally "blow against the state," used to describe a takeover of the government that is usually effected with sudden violence and armed forces.
East African High Commission	A British organization aimed at unifying the agricultural, health-care, and communications services of British-controlled Uganda, Kenya, and Tanganyika. The commission was disbanded when the former territories gained independence.
Kabaka	The Buganda word for "king."
Kanga **cloth**	Inexpensive cloth woven in Jinja and used for dressmaking by Ugandan women. Often printed with African proverbs, it is sold in large pieces.
Kanzu	A traditional garment, resembling a long nightshirt, that is still worn by Ugandan men in rural locations.

Kwashiorkor	A disease caused by lack of protein in the diet. Its symptoms are swelling of the arms, legs, and stomach and blotching of the skin's pigment.
Matoke	Fried balls of banana pulp, wrapped in banana leaves and usually served with fish or porridge.
Nagana	A disease of domestic animals caused by the bite of the tsetse fly.
National Resistance Army	A guerrilla movement against the Obote government in the early 1980s. President Museveni was a leader of the National Resistance Army.
Nationalization	The process of transferring all or part of the ownership of industry or property to the state. Nationalization is usually part of a Socialist system of government.
Polygamy	The practice of marriage by one man to more than one woman. Polygamy is practiced in many African countries and in Islamic cultures all over the world.
Posho	Porridge made from corn meal and water.
Protectorate	The status of a country or territory partially controlled, but not owned, by a dominant country.
Suspension of Political Activities Decree	An act, declared by Idi Amin in March 1971, that drastically curtailed the civil rights of Ugandan citizens.
Tsetse fly	A large fly that lives in brush and thickets in some parts of Africa. Its painful bite transmits the often-fatal sleeping sickness to humans and the disease nagana to domestic animals.
Ugandan National Liberation Front (UNLF)	An anti-Amin group formed by Ugandan exiles in Tanzania during the 1970s. The UNLF took control of the Ugandan government in 1979.
Uhuru	Swahili for "independence."

◄ I N D E X ►

ACKNOWLEDGMENTS

The author and publisher are grateful to the following sources for photographs: The New York Public Library (pp. 28, 32–33); The United Nations (pp. 34, 58, 63, 70, 72, 74, 76–77, 82–83, 84, 86, 88); The World Bank (p. 2); Smithsonian Institution Photographic Service (pp. 24–25); Photo Researchers, Inc. (pp. 39, 49, 50a, 50b, 51a, 51b, 52, 53, 54, 56, 66, 80); Taurus Photos, Inc. (pp. 42–43); The Bettmann Archive (pp. 54–55); Sygma (p. 46); Dennis Degnan (pp. 14, 18, 26, 53); Pictorial Parade/London Daily Express (pp. 21, 60–61); AP/Wide World Photos (pp. 16, 37, 44). Picture research: Maggie Berkvist, Susan Holtz.